MW00624307

MIRACLE
of
TITHING

৶

A Little Book of Answers to
Questions about Tithing

Mark Victor Hansen

M.V. Hansen & Associates, Inc.
Newport Beach, California
www.markvictorhansen.com

[handwritten signature and inscription across page]

P.S. I want to expand this...

Cataloging-in-Publication data is on file with
The Library of Congress
Library of Congress Control Number 2002115432

Hansen, Mark Victor
The Miracle of Tithing / Mark Victor Hansen
2002115432

© 2003 Mark Victor Hansen
ISBN 1-878549-05-7
Printed in the U.S.A.

Publisher:
M.V. Hansen & Associates, Inc
P.O. Box 7665
Newport Beach, CA 92658-7665
949.764.2640
www.markvictorhansen.com

Table of Contents

Chapter Three – How to Tithe

Chapter Four – To Whom Do I Tithe?

Other Works by Mark Victor Hansen

Books

The One Minute Millionaire:
The Enlightened Way to Wealth

The ever-expanding *Chicken Soup for the Soul* series

The Power of Focus

Future Diary

The Aladdin Factor: How to Ask for
and Get Everything You Want

Dare to Win

Treasury of Quotes

Out of the Blue, Delight Comes into Our Lives

Audio Programs

Dreams Don't Have Deadlines

How to Think Bigger Than
You Ever Thought You Could Think

The Aladdin Factor

Mastermind Your Way to Millions

Sell Yourself Rich

MEGA Book Marketing University

Special Reports & E-Booklets

Creating the Dream Team Advantage

Story-Board Your Future

There's No Such Thing as Failure

How to Veer from the Beaten Path

Focus on Your Primary Aim

Rejecting Rejection

Available for purchase at
www.markvictorhansen.com
Or by calling (800) 433-2314

❧

*Dedicated to shifting the awareness
of tithers and future tithers everywhere.*

❧

Introduction

In this book, I want to share a principle that creates miracles for me. It can do the same for you. The principle I am speaking of is tithing.

Tithing is the best-kept abundance and prosperity secret in existence. It's an old secret that works - yet has been virtually forgotten, never learned, or rarely tested. And, it's a sensitive subject. Ask most people about their giving and you'll likely hit a "hot button" as money is one of the last taboos.

I want you to understand and fully comprehend this great principle, as it will open life's cornucopia of unlimited good for you.

I believe we are each coded in our DNA to give. The more you give, the more fully you live. Tithing or giving is intrinsically a spiritual concept, where you're giving to your church, temple or spiritual home. However, I want this concept and book to be comfortable to the majority of people out there – especially you. If you're not connected with a church – if this type of tithing does not fit your experience – I encourage you to STILL tithe to a charity, cause or philanthropic organization that you can wholeheartedly support. Tithing is about making a difference in the world and, as a result, differences occur in your own life.

Earlier in my life, I had heard this life-giving principle lamely discussed and, though it perked my interest, I felt I was not financially comfortable enough to make the commitment. I had failed to understand the true significance of tithing. Most people plan to tithe after they have met all their other needs, but that's completely backwards to spiritual and universal law. Instead, you must tithe FIRST and then all your needs will be met!

Of course, I didn't realize this truth until it was too late. In 1974, I went bankrupt. I was mentally, spiritually and emotionally depressed. Finally, I decided to seek and find the prosperity principles, which I wrote into my book, *How to Achieve Total Prosperity*. While looking for principles that can work for anyone and everyone, I discovered "The Law of Tithing." I started by giving a little and kept increasing it as my returns increased in virtually automatic, invisible and often unexpected ways.

Tithing miracles never cease to amaze me. I expect them, and their consistent arrival is always delightful and fun to experience. For example my wife, Patty, and I re-financed an income-producing house at a high interest rate. We tithed on the $60,000 of equity borrowed because we saw it as true income. The banker called us unexpectedly almost immediately after we had tithed $6,000, and offered us alternative financing at a lower rate.

This saved us two points. A point is $1,000 per hundred borrowed, so we saved $2,000 immediately and, over a 30-year loan, saved $60,000 – that's tenfold what we tithed. It was a wonderful benefit and one we spiritually discerned.

"God my father has changed my wages 10 times."
Genesis 31:41

To give another example; as a professional speaker, I discovered that one dubious promoter bilked my colleagues out of fees, although he had paid me in full. This further assured me that tithing works invisibly because "God sees all."

I have reams of similar stories. These events could be called circumstance or coincidence, but I choose to believe that "right" giving and an "attitude of gratitude" means a great deal to God, and ultimately and inevitably, your mental, spiritual and physical returns are going to exceed any investment you make. This has been my experience. As John Marks Templeton, the billionaire founder of The Templeton Fund, the Young President's Club and the prestigious Templeton Award states, "Tithing always pays the best R.O.I. (Return on Investment)!"

This is the second edition of *Miracle of Tithing.* You're not going to believe what you read! I first wrote this as a booklet on tithing in 1984 because I was asked to do so by a great minister friend, who knows that my wife, Patty, and I believed in tithing, practiced it faithfully, and were harvesting its rich results.

Since its publication, my life has taken on even greater dimensions of grace, abundance and exceeding bounty that nurtures and blesses us. I can't even begin to tell you what kind of gratitude I feel daily for the life I now live. I know that these enhancements in my life are solely due to the "gratitude giving" in which Patty and I continue to participate.

In fact, as I was writing, *The One Minute Millionaire* with Bob Allen, we decided to inspire the creation of one million millionaires in a decade that also create an extra million each to give as a form of tithe. Imagine how that will shift our world!

I've learned a great deal about tithing in the last 30 years, and felt led to update this book. This time, however, I asked several thousand of my "Rich Results" e-zine readers (you can sign up too, at www.markvictorhansen.com) to participate in a survey of tithing questions. In just hours after sending the first "blast," we were bombarded with answers. Hundreds and hundreds more began responding from all parts of the globe – it was overwhelming and incredibly gratifying. It took us ALL by surprise!

With answers came questions, and we turned

those questions out again to the same readers, whether tithers or non-tithers, to hear their take on these subjects. Through it all, my team and I have sifted, sifted, and sifted some more to gather the stories, answer the questions, and share with you just a portion of the spiritual, mental and physical abundance my readers have shared with me.

This rewrite has been one of the most fascinating projects we've yet undertaken. It has altered our very lives as we've put it together for you.

Thank you to those of you who participated. I wish we could have included all your stories and comments. And thank you, reader, for wanting to learn more. This book is very capable of changing your life. Why? Because principles like tithing work for anyone who truly understands them.

Before you begin the short Question-and-Answer chapters themselves, I'd like you to read the first story on the next page. I've "book ended" the chapters of this book with readers' stories that absolutely tell the tale of what tithing can do in one's life. When you read this first story, I think it will help you better absorb and understand what follows.

Mark Victor Hansen
March 2003

Stephany's Story

Four years after my separation from my husband, I was in the process of attempting to set up a new business when I discovered that my partner had never filed our taxes.

I was faced with the challenge of recreating six to eight years worth of financial history, which was very costly in time and accountant's fees. In fact, my accountants from the beginning had explained that bankruptcy would make more sense for a fresh start. Since I considered myself responsible and one who always repaid her debts, I made the decision to "gut it out" and be responsible for whatever the outcome.

Two years later the provincial government decided to audit my returns for two of the six years. I cooperated considering it a routine formality.
But weeks dragged into months and I became frustrated. It was driving me crazy not knowing the full amount I was going to owe, never mind

the fact that my low-income, high debt circumstance made the thought of repayment impossible.

When I finally had the courage to inquire why the delay, the auditor told me quite frankly, "Well, it's your charitable donations we question."

I said, "Surely, you've run into people who tithe to their church and give to charity before. I've submitted official receipts. What is so strange about that?"

She replied, "Well, we would like further proof, perhaps cancelled checks, that this money was indeed given. It seems you've given too much! In fact, your donation levels are red flagged because they far surpass the average threshold for donations. Bluntly, it's hard to believe you've given such a high percentage of your income."

I laughed incredulously, "I'm being audited because I've given too much? Look, this has been a two year process, so please finish this audit and let me move on."

Another few months of hand wringing on government time, waiting for the verdict of how much I would owe. I held faith and prayed for a miracle. I envisioned the best-case scenario – maybe I'd have tax credits that would

cancel debt from other years, leaving me with a
reasonable and manageable amount to repay over time.

I confess, although I still tithed, each time I wrote a check
I hesitated, "Imagine being persecuted for giving too
much," I thought.

"Maybe I should give less!" Of course, I rejected
the thought as ridiculous and tithed anyway.

The lesson came the day I went to the bank to deposit
some money. I had received week's worth of very
confusing government notices with figures listing many
thousands of dollars. There were so many adjustments –
one department crediting and adjusting another, the
figures seemed one big blur. I had resolved to just save
money and let the accountants figure it all out.

When the bank clerk handed me my updated bankbook, I
gasped in disbelief. "Surely that balance could not be
right," I thought. Out loud, I said, "Please help me. There
has been a terrible error! It seems there is about $10,000
too much in my bank account. I'm sure it belongs to
someone else!"

After a flurry of activity between managers, it was
confirmed – it was a deposit from a special family tax
credit department. The tax department had calculated an

*additional and special child tax benefit, a sort of
government tax tithe to give families a break.
Although I was only entitled by law to eleven months
retroactive payment, by some miracle of
grace, someone, somewhere had made the generous
decision to credit me retroactive to the time my daughter
was born.*

*I received six years worth of payments at once. It was
more than enough to make a substantial dent in my debt,
relieve pressure, and answer my prayer for a reasonable
and manageable amount to repay.*

*Today, I am financially stable, have great
credit, and am on the path to creating a multi-million
dollar business. I am motivated by the thought of being
able to tithe more and make a significant difference,
thanks to this unforgettable lesson. I could think of no
better way for God to show me the grace and miracle
of tithing.*

*- **Stephany Crowley***

Chapter One

Why We Are Commanded to Tithe

What exactly is tithing?

෴ Tithing involves giving 10% of your income, regardless of where that income comes from. So, if you earn $100 a week, your weekly tithe would be $10. Earn $1,000 and your week's tithe would be $100; earn $10,000 weekly and your tithe would be $1,000.

When tithing is mentioned, most will point to the Bible's Old Testament.

> *Bring the whole tithe into the storehouse, so that there may be food in My house, and test me now in this, says the Lord of hosts, If I will not open for you the windows of heaven, and pour out for you a blessing until it overflows.*
> – Malachi 3:10
> (New American Standard Bible)

When you tithe, you experience a positive difference in your life. This is not because you're "bribing" God or manipulating God into a "quid pro quo" kind of situation. When you tithe, you're demonstrating an understanding of spiritual truths and the Universal Laws, both of which I'll be addressing in this book. Until people are spiritually and mentally awake to these truths, no education, social reform, or political reform will do any lasting good.

Why is a tithe one-tenth?
Why not one-sixteenth, one-eighth
or one-fourth?

❧ The actual definition of "tithe" IS ten! In fact, tithe is the old ordinal numeral in English. Changes in pronunciation in the prehistory of English are responsible for it looking so different from the word ten, but the two words are actually one and the same.

How would my piddly 10% have anything to do with The Big Picture?

❧ Your tithe is "seed money" for the world's greater good. You've probably heard tales of deep-water wells that have to be primed in order to get the water flowing. "Neighborly law" expects that every user pumps out what he or she needs and leaves a bucketful behind to seed the next flow of water.

Applied to this analogy, the tithing result is the actual well itself. It freely exists for all to regularly use – it keeps on giving. Your "seed" t ithe just helps start the flow. At the same time, while you are giving out of your reserve, you will never see the "well" in your life go dry. In fact, in many cases, your reserve grows, multiplies and expands automatically.

When we all do a little, a lot gets done. Your 10% matters – first to you (because God sees all) and second as it multiplies and serves others – both known and unknown to you.

Is tithing encouraged throughout the Bible?

❧ The Bible repeatedly prescribes tithing in the Old and New Testaments. It encourages each person to make tithing a cornerstone in his or her life.

A few examples from the Old Testament:

And all the tithe of the land, whether of the seed or the land, or of the fruit of the tree, is the Lord's: it is holy unto the Lord.
— Leviticus 27:30

Honor the Lord with thy substance, and with the first fruits of their increase, so shall thy barns be filled with plenty, and thy presses shall burst with new wine."
— Proverbs 3:10

When Jacob had a vision of a ladder reaching into Heaven, he committed himself to the practice of tithing, realizing that; "God will be with me, and will keep me in the way that I go, and will give me bread to eat and raiment to put on so that I come again to my father's house in peace."

And let's not forget the entire book of Job, which demonstrates selfless tithing, giving and faith in the face of great hardship.

In the New Testament, Jesus repeatedly pointed out the gift of tithing, regardless how small, in actual events and parables such as the boy's gift of fish to feed thousands, or the instance of a widow giving a lowly mite.

Tithing is essential to the development of the soul. In fact, I believe you can look at your giving in your checkbook and it is a great barometer of your soul's development, evolution and growth. God wants you to tithe and experience abundance freedom so you can apply your new time freedom to experience relationship freedom, soul freedom, and the ability to persistently employ your full genius freedom! You're here to grow and be free!

Is it true that most of the Bible's heroes are men and women of wealth?

It is absolutely true that Moses, Abraham, Isaac, Joseph, Jacob, David, Solomon, Rebecca and others, prospered greatly. God rewards individuals for wisely employing and maximizing their resources while expressing an attitude of gratitude and thankfulness. Do you remember the parable of the talents? A rich landowner gave a talent to each of his servants before beginning his travels. One buried the talent for safekeeping, another spent it haphazardly, and the third invested it wisely to produce greater income for his master. When you "bury your talent," you are called "weak and slothful." When you multiply it, you are called "A good and faithful servant."

In Chapter 13 of Genesis, it is recorded that Abraham was *"very rich in cattle, silver, and in gold; thus fulfilling God's earlier promise…'and I will bless you and make you great.'"* Each of us can personalize and individualize God's promise to Abraham as our own valuable and viable affirmation. In your deep meditations hear God tell you, **"…and I will bless you and make you great."**

Isaac is described in the 26th chapter of Genesis, as having *"possessions of flocks and possessions of herds and much wealth."*

In the 29th chapter of Chronicles, the narrative tells of David's gifts toward the construction of the temple, including one million talents of gold, two million talents of silver, and precious stones and pearls. Then the chiefs of the tribes matched these gifts with some of their own: five thousand talents of gold, twenty thousand talents of tin as well as brass and iron.

David truly understood how to use wealth wisely by *"seeking first the Kingdom"* and *"having all (good) things added unto him."* David told Solomon, *"And keep the charge of the Lord and walk in his ways and keep his statutes… that you may prosper in all that you do and succeed wherever you go."* (This last phrase would also be excellent to memorize and meditate on as your own truth.) Solomon obviously accepted this idea because he went on to become the richest man in the world at that time.

Curiously, two of the richest men in America (Bill Gates, the computer software genius behind Microsoft, and Warren Buffet, America's most profitable investor, have both promised, written in their wills and already begun establishing foundations that allow them to give 99% of their wealth to causes in which they believe in.

What does all this mean? From Biblical times to present day, people who recognize and utilize the spiritual truth of tithing <u>do not lose</u>. They are safe and protected in their faith.

Will you have unlimited good at your beck and call all the time? Will your head be heaped with gold when you begin to tithe? No, there's no promise of all times good or super wealth showing up at your doorstep. But, you'll find in the pages ahead, strange and wonderful things do begin to happen to people who faithfully, continuously and substantially tithe! It's a marathon, not a short race.

Is tithing like a bargain with God? If I do this good for God, will it be returned in greater amounts and supply?

🔊 In my opinion, tithing is not a bargaining chip or, as one of my readers noted, "a nasty way to put God on the hook to reciprocate." This "reciprocation concept" is taught extensively around the world and, unfortunately, is sometimes taught more rigorously by people who mean no good will for us or our tithes.

God demanded tithing but he gave us free will to comply or not comply. If we don't comply, He doesn't love us any less. He just lovingly knows we can do better.

After all, no matter what our temporary stories or struggles, we are surrounded by a world's abundance each and every day. Tithing takes off our blinders so we can see God's great and generous abundance. If you can rise above the stories and struggles for just a moment, I'm sure you'll begin to recognize that you, too, have abundance in *every* facet of your life.

When I tell you that tithers enjoy a greater, more abundant life, it's not because God necessarily "chose" to throw brightness in their lives while leaving non-tithers in the dark...it's because tithers have made a decree of spirit and from *this* spirit, their worlds open and brighten. Life and its experiences can only go up from there.

Will you receive in return? Absolutely, but this is not what should be motivating you to tithe. It is important to do it because it feels *right*. Tithing is a thanksgiving, a gift of gratitude that can be shared with your fellow man. By fulfilling the Law of Tithing, you inevitably demonstrate gratitude for the abundance, prosperity, "have-ness" surplus and plenty in your life. Thought combined with feeling through tithing guarantees that abundance, confidence, faith and trust will increase by leaps and bounds in return.

From My Readers

If we begin from the position that everything belongs to God, the question of tithing becomes one of stewardship rather than legal conformity or inducing God's favor. How I use the things He has entrusted to me is important because my actions will show either God's presence or His absence in my life.

- Mark Walker

In a nutshell, what is the purpose of tithing?

∞ Every individual's purpose in tithing is to open up his/her awareness of spiritual truth and Universal Laws. Tithing helps you to truly know yourself. Tithing turns on the spigot of all good!

As you tithe for you, your family, your future and to better thank and comprehend a loving and generous supply, you'll find yourself moving into the fourth dimension of love and the spiritual truth of tithing wholeness which is unavailable to the unenlightened.

From My Readers

Tithing isn't about giving money away. Tithing is about trusting completely in something outside of yourself, something more powerful than you could ever be or imagine, that has your best interest at heart. Tithing is about giving yourself away, only to receive a bigger you back. Tithing is about looking beyond your own pain and hurts and helping others. It's about sharing everything of you, and having everything in the world returned to you. Tithing is trust, love, compassion ...in essence, it is life magnified.

- Lisa Vaden

Chapter Two

How Tithing Changes Us

What are the Universal Laws, and how do they work with tithing?

❧ Since the beginning of time, certain universal "truths" were set in motion that provide a constant, uniform and orderly method to the way the world works. These laws work in and around us, no matter what we do or how we think. They are:

The Law of Energy Becoming Reality – Energy moves into physical form. What you give out in energy (your tithe) materializes in physical results.

The Law of Vibration/Attraction – Everything in the universe vibrates, nothing rests. Your thoughts and subsequent actions are vibrations that you send off into the universe which, in turn, attract like-minded energy and vibration to you.

The Law of Relativity – Nothing is good or bad until it's compared to something. For instance, some people may have greater abundance and prosperity than you and, likewise, you have more than another person.

The Law of Polarity – Everything has an opposite. If something bad happens in your life, there has to be something good about it. It's *how* you look at the situation that makes it good or bad.

Remember this as you begin to tithe, no matter what your situation.

The Law of Rhythm – The tide goes in, the tide goes out. When you're on a down swing, know that the tide will be changing – it's a law. " And this too shall pass."

The Law of Gestation – Every "seed" has a gestation period. Manifestation into form or physical results is guaranteed to occur when the time is right. If you don't experience immediate changes in your life because of tithing, remember this law.

And, lastly, what I consider to be the most important universal law for tithing:

The Law of Cause and Effect – What you send into the Universe comes back to you. There is no such thing as chance. Everything happens according to Law and nothing ever escapes the Law. When you give back 10% of your income, you will set this divine Law into motion – Question is, will you be ready to receive?

Will tithing change my attitude about money specifically?

✎ Actually, yes. Without a doubt, tithing breaks addiction to money!

So many people are caught up in the idea that money is actually an object that can be handled and manipulated and, thus, be noticeably absent from one's life. But, if you read the Universal Laws above, you should now understand that money is just energy that happens to move into physical form. But, because money is just energy to begin with, understand that you have a great deal of power in utilizing, attracting and controlling that energy into your life with The Law of Vibration/Attraction.

Tithing helps you gain a better understanding of "energy in motion" that both works for a greater good and goes out to the universe to inevitably return to you.

I know of a millionaire friend who actually dives into his pocket on occasion, pulls a bill from his money clip and, without even looking at its currency, throws it from his car window or drops it on a sidewalk! Now, without going into the definition of "tithing" in this rather odd sense, he is absolutely clear on one thing: When he's able to remove money from his person (and considerably brighten the day of an innocent passerby) he truly understands that money is simply an energy that he can easily release because it will easily find its way to him again.

My attitude has improved considerably and tithing comes quite easily now. I hold on less tightly to money and feel that more is right around the corner.

- David Berquist

What are the spiritual and emotional "wins" I'll experience from tithing?

1. Tithing asserts that you're not the source. The only source and supply of all good is God. Everything you give cements the belief that you are not the Creator of your circumstances, that you are a fortunate recipient of God's gracious universe. This is where tithing starts. Customers, clients, employers, employees, family members, spouses, siblings, and your own children are all instruments through which God's supply is being channeled.

2. Tithing opens your heart to greater good. Goodness can't come into your life until you open

Tithing and giving have impact because they change us, not God. We understand that we are not the center of the universe, we give from what we have been given, and we share as the recipients of God's blessings, not to induce it.

- Mark Walker

A few years ago, I was sitting in a mechanic's shop with an over-heated Volvo, lamenting over our new business, our low funds for our living expenses, and our daughter in college...(You get the picture.) While waiting for the mechanic, I opened my glove compartment and found my pastor's book about spiritual principles as they relate to stress.

I turned to the chapter about money and tithing, and I finally got it: The truth about tithing for me is the recognition that God is the source of my supply! I finally understood that money is simply a means of exchange and operates as energy that flows for the substance we all deserve.

We tithe to say, "We'll give back 10% and trust and have faith that you will provide what we need. Not just money, but everything we need." Boy, do we have a testimony.

Since we started tithing regularly, we have manifested the ownership of a Ford dealership; the next year, a Lincoln-Mercury dealership. I wanted to travel. We travel. We wanted to pay our bills. We pay them, now with a smile. We give our spirits and love to everyone we meet. We give money to family and friends, to folks in front of Wal-Mart, and we tip people really well. Our hands are open because we know the hand that is open to us will never close.

- Vicki Goldston

your doors of giving. Tithing works because it works from inside you. There is only one "door knob" on the door of your heart – only you can use free will to open that door and give. When you open the door to your heart, everything changes your belief and a new understanding coming about giving. Giving assures receiving. It always has and it always will. What is amazing is that giving expands your spirituality, especially when you give in the spirit of love, joy, and cheerfulness from an unselfish heart.

3. Tithing demonstrates faith and trust beyond fear.

You've heard it said before: "You're given a fear so that you'll be able to walk through it."

I find that when I give with faith and joy in the abundance of the universe, my life is filled with abundance. When I am worried and fearful and hoard the money, my life reflects that, too. It is a visible ebb and flow connected to fear and worry vs. faith and joy.

- Elizabeth Madsen

What I have noticed – when I tithe from the spirit of it being from abundance, there is always enough, no matter how much I give. When I am afraid and fear I'm outside my "comfort zone," then I've experienced some pretty tight months.

- Tina Fox

I think in every tither's life, there comes a moment of truth when we have to decide about walking through that fear; we have to decide to rely on something other than our own human ability to provide. We have to step out on

God's ability.

Fear of poverty causes people to stay impoverished and immobilized. Tithing with head faith and heart faith prevents the disease called poverty by creating a state of mental, spiritual and financial prosperity.

In the Old Testament, Job said, *"The thing I have so greatly feared has come upon me."* God was asking Job to walk through his fear. Job kept having faith and kept tithing even when his wife and family told him he was nuts. They believed that God had forsaken him, but Job knew better. He hung in there and for that faith, he was richly rewarded. Even when you can't see the light at the end of the tunnel, have faith. Remember, *"Faith is the substance of things hoped for, and evidence of things not seen."*

Faith is substantial. It's real, or becoming real. We see that our intangible dreams with faith become our tangible and substantial reality. That's why Jesus said, *"You'll know their faith by their results."*

4. Tithing teaches you that service always comes before rewards.

You have to dig the well before you can drink...you have to pave the highway before you can travel...you have to chop the wood before you get the heat. Many people on this planet think just the opposite – they have a high expectation to be served and, therefore, never experience the reality of a life they've desired. You've already been richly rewarded...now give back through joyful tithing and giving of service and you will be rewarded.

Here's an extreme story – or at least, it seems extreme until you begin to see what tithing does in your own life.

At one point in his life, my dear friend Chip Collins, a professional speaker and trainer who helped me begin my speaking career, was down to his last 35 cents. He had a wife and a baby to feed at home and no hope of earning any money that day or week. With tears in his eyes, he started beating on his steering wheel saying, "God, what should I do?" Intuition flared and told him to tithe.

He figured 35 cents would not even buy milk for his baby, so he went into a nearby Catholic Church and prayerfully put 35 cents in the offering plate with thanks to God for all that he'd received and enjoyed in his life. As he walked out of the church, he still remembers the peace he felt. Within steps of the church, a gentleman approached him and said, "Chip, a few months ago, you solicited me for a talk to my real estate agents and I want to hire you."

Chip was hired and prepaid the $200 fee that day, which saved his family from lack,

limitation, hunger and deprivation. It also re-
established his self-esteem as a good provider.
He has since never swayed from being a disciplined
and committed tither.

Your needs and mine exist to be met, not to
intimidate, embarrass and harass us.

**5. Tithing allows you to discover and utilize
your own unique talents.**

Each of us has a magnificent (and usually
invisible) talent that we're asked to recognize and
maximize by giving it away. A perfect example of
one such individual who's utilizing her talents for
the better good is Oprah Winfrey.

Oprah has unselfishly given of herself to make
the world a better place. She has been in movies,

TV and radio and does talks around the country. She saw what Paul Newman did with Newman's Own salad dressings and sauces (giving over $150 million to countless charities) and has, in turn, created a cosmetics company that is destined to do the same. She has tithed her spirit, mind, and body and even convinced her show-business friends to do the same. As a result, she has been universally loved, respected, appreciated and admired. Oprah is a classical "Resource Philanthropist," who has used her own gifts to create other gifts that are forever giving. Her phenomenal example is an inspiration.

6. Your life-force energy actually increases by giving.

All great people are givers. They give 100% of themselves to whatever project they approach. I just mentioned Oprah and she's one of hundreds you know who are recognized now for what they give rather than for what they get in life...people like Bob Hope, Paul and Joann Newman, Pam and Ed McMann, Linda and Millard Fuller (co-founders of Habitat for Humanity)...the list goes on and on. Make the giving principle real and personal in your life by testing it against every need you have – mentally, physically, financially, socially or spiritually. These principles have never failed me, they've never failed the folks I've just mentioned, and they will not fail you.

7. You become solution-oriented rather than problem-oriented.

This is a mystical and unexplainable phenomena that just happens, and it happens on two levels – it happens personally in your own life, and it happens as you reach out to help the world around you. Remember, the Law of Relativity says there's always something better and something worse than your current situation. There's always someone doing better and someone doing worse than you. By tithing, you come to understand the Law of Relativity and how you, yourself, can create change in the universe. You are the change you seek. When you tithe, it transforms you as assuredly as the caterpillar morphs into a butterfly.

In addition to my regular tithing, I give to individuals as they are brought into my life. The amounts have varied from $100 dollars to $2,500 dollars. I live in Idaho and work trade shows in most of the larger cities in the West. Two years ago, a single female friend with a 14-year-old son living in Seattle called and told me that her ex-boyfriend had broken into her home and stolen $2,500 dollars from her. She didn't ask for money, just needed a friend to listen. She is self-employed with a cleaning service and two employees. This money was needed to pay her employees and her bills. The weekend after her call, I was scheduled to do a trade show at the Portland Expo. Later that week, I detoured through Seattle on my way to Portland and gave my friend $2,500 dollars. This was not a loan, but a gift that I knew God wanted me to offer in His name.

My normal retail gross sales at the Portland trade show would usually average $9000 for the weekend. That weekend – the weekend after giving this monetary gift – my retail sales at Portland was $16,000 dollars. This is one of many examples of tithing that has happened several times in my life.

- A.T. Blann

What is "manifestation consciousness" and how does it apply to tithing?

❧ Manifestation consciousness occurs when you understand that something can be manufactured out of nothing (Remember the Law of Energy Becoming Reality: Energy perpetually moves into physical form). The intangible becomes tangible and **you can facilitate that whole invisible network with your tithing.** Once you tithe, you're increasing energy's flow and movement immediately. It begins to manifest instantly in the real world.

This same "law" can be applied to how you THINK about tithing. Your thoughts create. They are simply a higher form of energy that moves into form to create your reality around you. So, in actuality, your thoughts are things. When you're thinking lack, you stay in lack. When you're thinking abundance, you attract abundance. As I mentioned in a recent interview with my friend, Mike Littman, "prosperity" is a Latin word that means, "Be in the flow." Every one of us can be in the flow when we are thinking right, talking right, acting right, and living right. We get the right results right here, right now.

So, when you're tithing, is it more important WHAT you tithe, or HOW you tithe?

❧ Without a doubt, it's more important HOW you tithe. What kind of a person are you when you tithe? How are you showing up? Being always precedes doing and having. The law is Be – Do – Have, not the other way around!

A tither who gives in a stingy or begrudging manner receives in a stingy, begrudging manner. This doesn't have anything to do with God; it's not a punishment – it's simply the Law of Cause and Effect! His or her Scrooge-like attitude and disposition will give him or her drab returns in many facets of life.

When you don't give spiritually with a joyous heart, your life automatically contracts. In fact, in most cases, it manifests the most negativity when you're in the direst of straits.

I know of a man who claims he has been "forced" into tithing. Right now, he enjoys newfound wealth beyond his wildest dreams, but he doesn't recognize the correlation between the people around him who instigated the tithe, and this change in his life. In just the last year alone, I've seen his whole life begin to shut down and crush down on him. He's losing his health, his family, and his friends, even his work.

Is this coincidence? Absolutely not. This man is losing because he's violating spiritual truth and Universal Law.

Tithing should never be done with a sense of superstition or with any misgiving, fear, guilt or shame with any misgivings. Such negative states of consciousness preclude any demonstration of prosperity.

You've got to stop operating at a low, needy level. This mindset "freezes" you and eliminates your abundant future. You've got to ascend – and the only way to ascend is to "heat up!" There's nothing better for a frozen life than the heat spark produced when you begin to tithe.

Think of it this way – when a frozen pond begins to thaw from heat, the water begins to move. As the energy starts flowing in those water molecules, the water itself will create faster thaw across the pond. Were the water to heat to boiling, it becomes vapor and expands even further. The energy around tithing works in this very same fashion. Tithing is an extremely efficient and effective act-of-faith. The practice of tithing will deepen your whole-hearted feeling and conviction that it works as life changes pour into your experience.

Chapter Three

How to
Tithe

If there were a set-in-stone, absolutely-no-question way to tithe, I'd be telling you about it. While there are certainly guidelines, we have freedom to move within the parameters of tithing.

I've never tithed before and, admittedly, still feel some reluctance. How do you recommend I start?

✆ If you have never tried tithing, give it a six month trial period. After that, I know you will never question its validity again. You will tithe forever. As you do it, it will become more effortless and easy as it develops into your most positive habit.

If I have cash flow now and don't tithe, what happens?

✆ Remember always: *"God is the source and supply of all good."*

If we don't tithe, it means either we are ignorant of the law of tithing, we don't believe in God's law, or we don't believe in the universal laws on which our planet relies.

If you know you should tithe and don't, you will reap in experience what you sow in consciousness.

Just as I explained in the previous chapter, this

is not a punishment, it is simply law. When you close up, the world closes up around you. You may stay "stuck," or you may even lose what you have or its abundant flow. Am I saying this to scare or threaten you? Of course not. I'm simply telling you how law – which governs everything inside and around us – works.

It's like the automobile driver who knows the car needs oil and does not put it in. Sooner or later, the car stalls, comes to a screeching halt and requires expensive attention to get it back into working mode. It would have taken just a couple $2 cans of oil to keep that car running at maximum efficiency, but the driver chose consciously to ignore the way the car's engine is set up, the car's "law," so to speak. Once the oil ran dry, a chain of cause-and-effect reactions began to play out.

Material prosperity – no matter how vast – inevitably stalls unless spiritual prosperity ensures its sacred flow through regular, automatic, systematic tithing.

Should I make tithing a lifelong habit?

🪝 Absolutely, yes! Tithing is easy if it becomes a regular and systematic habit. Give 10% of your income and live on the remaining 90%. The first 10% is given back, and practiced tithers would never dream of hording any of it. They live in the principle and receive untold blessings, benefits and protection. They are devoted to giving, receive the returns, and are free from financial worries of destitution.

What happens if I give and don't receive?

෨ First and foremost, tithing does not always return in material fashion. If you're expecting to win the Lotto, get an insurance windfall or have your mortgage company unexpectedly offer to pay off your house just because you put money in the offering plate last week, you've got the wrong mindset about tithing. **Tithing isn't about getting back – it's about expressing gratitude and giving back and/or paying forward.**

At the same time, and from my own experience, if you show me a person having financial difficulties, I'll show you a non-tither or a tither with a bad attitude. I know thousands of tithers and every one of them has more than they require in life. Tithers may have other problems but they never are in want.

When people ask me this question, I tell them to check themselves out with this simple test:

1. Do I recognize that there is a greater source and supply of all good?

2. Am I tithing regularly and with a system? Do I tithe when I receive income of any kind, at the beginning of projects and at their successful conclusion?

3. What is my attitude about tithing? What are the emotions I feel when I tithe?

4. Am I truly conscious to receive? Am I awake to all the possible channels that are trying to give me surplus good? Do I listen to my still inner voice and intuitive hunches?

Write out your answers to these four questions privately, and then ask your spouse or someone close to you (someone you trust) to respond to the same questions. Also ask them to write about what they think you do within the above questions! It might prove very enlightening.

Do I have to start at 10%?

❧ Well, if you'll remember, the word "tithe" means "TEN," not four, not two-point-five, not seven-and-an-eighth, but TEN.

Many people stall on beginning to tithe because they really feel they can't give that 10%. So, don't. Start at 1% if you have to. But promise me this – promise yourself that you will build to 10% within a set timeframe (set that date now), as

I cannot tell you how blessed my husband and I have been since I began tithing. I just didn't think we could afford it, living on $25K a year. But I decided this: Money was going to four places each month - the mortgage company, the grocery, the power company, and the phone bill. I figured I could add tithing to that and not die...I'm in commission sales without a draw so I never know how much I'll have from check to check. When I first started, I just didn't think I could drop 10 % off the top right away, so I said, "Okay Lord, I don't think I can pull this off because I don't have enough faith to give up 10 %, but I do have enough to give up 5 %... no maybe 2 %. If you can prove to me that we'll still be fine, I'll give 5 % next month, and again until I can get up to 10 %" I look back now – three years later - and laugh! The day I gave that 2 % was on a Sunday. In Monday's mail, came TWICE the amount I'd just pledged from a source I'd never known existed...an escrow adjustment on my mortgage .Needless to say, the next month, the same thing happened – money came in from an unexpected freelance job. After that, I have stayed at giving 10 % of every check I get.

- Chris Wilson

has been commanded. The truth is: If you won't give ten cents out of a dollar, you won't give $100 out of $1,000. You have to start somewhere with something. Today.

> *If you give, you will get! Your gift will return to you in full and overflowing measure, pressed down, shaken together to make room for more, and running over. Whatever measure you use to give – large or small – will be used to measure what is given back to you.*
>
> — Luke 6:38 (LB)

Do I tithe gross or net from my income?

⋟ This was one of the most frequently asked questions from my readers who wrote in about tithing. From my own readings, research and conversations with theologians and philosophers, I personally believe you start with gross income – after all, this is the total abundance given you. In the past, my wife Patty and I have even tithed 10% from gross LOANS we've received and, I can assure you, not once has it ever proven detrimental.

Many people will tithe from their net income after taxes – so, they tithe 10% from their paycheck, period. If this makes you more comfortable, then do what makes you comfortable! Start where you believe and remember, "It comes unto you according to your belief." I'd encourage you to start with net and then, as you begin to see your life's resources grow, take the leap of faith and tithe from your gross. You'll be flabbergasted at what begins to occur in your life, all around you.

Because I received so many questions from my readers about gross/net, I went back to my readers and asked what they were actually practicing. Of the several hundred responses I received in return, "gross" led "net" by about a 2:1 ratio.

Read on, you may find yourself agreeing with or being drawn to one of my reader's excerpts.

If I write my tithe check after I've written half a dozen other checks, I believe I've put all of those others before God. That doesn't honor God. It may seem simple, but by writing out the check for the tithe before you write the check for rent or food or anything else, you've put God first and that means you've given Him permission to handle your income.

- Charlene McCulloch

Tithe gross. The Bible says we are to tithe our "first fruits." It doesn't say anything about "after taxes".

- Richard McGinn

One day when I was kidding with my minister father-in-law, I asked him if tithing 10% of your income meant 10% of the gross, or 10% of the net. He didn't take a second to answer. He smiled at me, looked me right in the eye and said, "Well, Janey, how much abundance do you want?

- Jane Willhite

As a CPA, I have been asked to help clients determine how much tithing they should pay. One individual, who was very well-to-do, said that it is easy to determine how to tell how much to pay. You simply look at the adjusted gross income line of your 1040 and apply the 10% to that figure.

- Dexter Snow

I now tithe from my personal gross. I know that I will always share the abundance I receive from Universal Source through my willingness to work smart and receive.

- Barbara Lepori Lundberg

Can I tithe more than 10%?

❧ Are you kidding? Of course you can! I have many close friends and associates who do just that. In fact, Dave Anderson, who co-founded the Rain Forest Café and Famous Dave's BBQ Ribs companies, does more than just provide 50,000 meals a day in America. Dave believes in a concept I call **Reverse Tithing** – he's enjoyed such natural and easy success that **he keeps 10% and gives 90% away...**and more keeps coming in the door! Dave says it has worked in both boom and recessionary times. The same amazing phenomenon is possible for you, too. Remember, it's not what you tithe but HOW you tithe. When you tithe with the proper attitude, lack ceases in your life.

On a more legal note, here in the United States, the IRS will allow tax credit for up to 50% on one's adjusted gross income, if given to religious and/or charitable enterprises.

Tithing is not and never has been an ending place. It is a beginning place. It stimulates the law of circulation to operate. A tithe is not a debt we owe, but a seed we sow!

How often do I need to tithe?

🪢 If I've heard it once, I've heard it a thousand times – consistency is the key here. **Whenever income arrives, tithe.**

If you receive a regular paycheck (even if it's an unemployment check or a welfare check), be sure to tithe every time that paycheck comes in. Some people even set up auto-debit from their checking accounts to take care of the tithe automatically. More and more churches and philanthropic organizations are utilizing this method to make it easier for tithers.

While I heartily encourage you to live solely from "real" money in your checking account and from your checking debit card, I've had readers tell me that they do auto-tithing from their interest-bearing credit cards as well. As long as you're paying off those monthly balances EVERY month, I think this is a great way to ensure consistent tithing. But, if you're running up interest dues because of debt on that credit card, better to remove your tithe completely to a more traditional check writing or cash tendered arena!

Perhaps you receive money on commissions or are an independent contractor who's paid on a project-only basis. As with people who receive regular paychecks, the same theory holds true: The best time to tithe is immediately upon receipt of income, whether daily, weekly, monthly or quarterly.

While some people do wait to tithe at the end of the year or fiscal year, it is easier for the majority of tithers to tithe a little at a time, as it arrives. It's harder when you choose to wait and attempt to make a big payment.

I will say that I have learned a couple lessons about tithing the hard way. First of all, I had to make a quality decision to consistently tithe and stick by it. Stopping and starting or being inconsistent in one's tithing will hinder one's prosperity.

I began tithing about ten years ago when I learned what the Word said about tithing. I was consistent in spite of circumstances for a long time and I began to increase. But I made some mistakes and things went from bad to really, really bad and I got lax in my tithing. I convinced myself that I only had to tithe on things I earned and not on everything I got, so my income went up and down constantly. That is, until I began to consistently tithe.

- Charlene McCullogh

I'd also encourage you away from "putting money away" to save as a lump-sum tithe. First, it's too easy to dip into should finances get a bit tight. Secondly, and most importantly, the world needs your tithe NOW – not a year from now. Remember the Law of Energy Becoming Reality – even a very small tithe, put out to the world as soon as income arrives, begins to manifest into physical form *immediately*.

Can I defer the payment of my tithe to a future time?

ᑐ Most individuals need the security of tithing in the sweet here and now to feel and know that their good is circulating freely. However, there are people who follow Andrew Carnegie's lead. As Carnegie began building his business, he made a written covenant saying, "I'll earn money the first half of my life and then attend to tithing and charity the second half of my life to do the most good and the least harm with my money."

Carnegie was the richest man of his time and gave Carnegie Hall, 3,000 libraries and a Foundation that does charitable acts to create peace and foster education for all. Perhaps your trust bond is this clear.

Henry Ford also had a prayerful "future income" covenant. His memoirs state that he asked

I've got a different approach to tithing. I've set up a foundation and, when I die, all my money goes to this foundation. All of it. My two daughters will be employed by the foundation at a reasonable salary to distribute the foundation's funds to worthwhile charities over a period of 20 years. Instead of giving 10% to charities, my foundation will give 90%.

Joe Sugarman

for help in realizing his fullest potential and he, in turn, would remember and over-tithe out of the ever-increasing future abundance. His Ford Foundation continues to help churches and funds foundations to this day.

The Rockefeller and Ford Foundations are both multi-billion dollar enterprises attempting to serve the health and educational needs of humanity's less fortunate people. Their foundations have left a lasting legacy. You can do the very same as long as you write out a goal to do so and take the action to obtain your desired result.

Do I tithe on my current or future income?

❧ Oddly (and quite unexpectedly), I received several stories from readers who had decided to tithe against what they had written as future goal income.

In my book, *Future Diary* (you can find it at http://www.markvictorhansen.com), I encourage you to write down whatever good you desire in the future. This should include your future income goals. Expand on that idea by writing down what you want to financially tithe, from the beginning through these expanded earnings.

Whether you tithe on current earnings, or decide to commit a little above and beyond your current income, is up to you. Whatever the case, this action gives you immediate direction and stair-step commitment to your tithing.

Whatever your great future gift (tithe) is to life, please write it down and make it clear. Perhaps you can make it so outrageously spectacular and life-benefiting that you can induce a veritable team of others to help you realize your dream.

My point is that you will pass a financial number in your future wealth where you have more than enough for all your needs. Plan now to create a foundation or trust to give away the unstoppable excess funds and make a lasting difference!

We are pastors of Church on the Rock in San Diego. We've had some wonderful testimonies this year, including: A woman tithed on what she wanted to earn instead of her regular salary for a year. At year's end, she had her annual review and received a $5,000 raise (bringing her up to the amount she wanted to receive and had been tithing.) Additionally, she received an unexpected $5,000 bonus.

— **John & Kathy Casto**

We were in the process of planting our vineyards and drilling for water. At 300 feet with not a drop of water to be found, the driller suggested we find another location. We had already spent thousands to drill to the point we were at. In bed that evening, I woke my fiancé, Darryl, and said I knew why we had not hit water...it was because we had not made a commitment to tithe from the vineyards. After a long discussion based on our expected returns per our business plan, we made a written decision on the amount we were to give and where to send it. You, of course, know the ending ...next day they drilled two feet and hit 352 gallons of water a minute. Our grapes continue to thrive and we are grateful.

— **Shirley Hunt**

I'm a small business owner.
How do I tithe personally?
Do I tithe from the business as well?

∿ As a reminder, there are many business structures out there (such as businesses with licensees or franchisees, or businesses that are publicly traded) that must follow specific regulations on "tithing." If you're the owner of such an entity, you know you have to check with more than one person (and at least your CPA) when you decide to tithe the business income! But, there are many sole proprietorships or small businesses that have every right and freedom to tithe in that business' behalf.

At my company, Mark Victor Hansen & Associates, Inc., my wife, Patty, and I tithe a percentage of the company's income to designated entities. As many of you may know, each of our *Chicken Soup for the Soul* books is also dedicated to giving a portion of its earnings to a specific charitable/non-profit entity. I am deeply thankful that my partner, Jack Canfield, my publisher, and co-authors are willing to selflessly contribute to mutually agreed-upon entities.

On a side note, I think that building your own business is a gift to the world because it requires you to tap in deep to your greatest resources, strengths and talents in order to provide a unique entity of service to the rest of the world. You've been blessed with unique gifts that no other business person could utilize in same manner, and you're able to give back to the world in such a unique way – what a great gift it is to be a business owner! Being successful is the most unselfish thing you can do. Why? Because each millionaire creates at least 10 new jobs. Now, how that's for a goal?)

In my opinion, I think it's important that you tithe both business AND personal income. After all, both your business and your personal income operate from the same single source of supply and for that you can feel honored and grateful.

Sometimes in the building and capitalization periods of a business, tithing from both entities can be a little difficult, particularly if you're trying to tithe gross income amounts. So, I'll revert to what I've instructed before: Tithe what you can.

When we were discussing this issue for the book, I suggested you first tithe from your personal income supplied by salary or personal loan payback through your business. Then, also tithe from the company's net until its assured growth allows you to tithe from a gross level.

I had many, many business owners chime in with their practices. If you're drawn to any one of these comments, I'd suggest that be the route you take in your own business life.

A business is designed to make an income. To tithe GROSS would pillage the business of its life-blood ... cash ... in huge amounts. No, tithing should be from the net product of the business, the net profit.

- Robert Jordan

Both. I am a separate entity from my business. My business can tithe to larger institutes and I get to tithe to smaller more personal causes. I want my business to tithe long after I'm gone. For some reason, doing this produces rewards unexpected yet appreciated, and always rewards the soul.

- Gordon Alexander

I am just starting with my own business, but my plan is to tithe from the business and from my personal income, too. I think that by doing that I am giving God the glory for how He blesses both my business and me.

- Lynn Bassett

The business is a separate entity if it is a corporation, and is considered able to make decisions and purchases by itself. With this in mind, if you are the owner of the business, your responsibility will be based off of any increases or profits that the business produces. This is in addition to any take home pay you may have. So, both the business profits and the take home pay are considered an increase and should have tithing taken from each."

- Enoch Bishop

I'm in the halfway zone between "net" and "gross" tithes on my business. The way I see it, my business provides livelihood to talented writers who have confidence and faith in our company's consistent growth and solidity. It's paramount to me that I keep them well paid and reward them for their impeccable work.

So, I created a spreadsheet – as soon as we bill on a contract, that expected gross income is entered in the spreadsheet, along with the payouts due my writers based on that contract. When the income arrives, I pay my writers immediately. At that net, I pay our tithe to the organization we've voted to support. Then I cover remaining expenses.

As a service-oriented business, it works perfectly for us, and I no longer worry about getting the bills paid, least of all my own salary. On the personal side, I tithe 10% from salary and dividends.

- Diane Armitage

I tithe on all the money I draw out of the business.

- Donna Gulley

It is required to tithe on your personal increase. Therefore it is not necessary to tithe twice – only on the amount you personally received.

- Gary Dixon

This question makes the concept of gross and net more relevant. In this case I would have to say choosing to use the net figure of business income is the most logical. A business might gross $1 million a year, but after expenses be left with only $150,000. To tithe 10% of gross ($100,000) would be very generous, but quite possibly impractical.

As they say, in business it's not what you earn, but what you keep. In this way, you could treat the money paid to yourself as an expense to the business (which it often is). Say you paid yourself a $50,000 salary from this business. This would reduce the net business income to $100,000. Now you could tithe 10% from the business and also 10% from your personal income. This would still yield a total combined giving of $15,000.

Businesses run as a sole proprietorship have less distinction between business and personal income, as the net income from the business is just added to your annual income for tax purposes. If our above example were again applied, we would end up with $150,000 in personal income, to which we could apply our 10% formula.

- Alex Mackenzie

My business tithes monthly as we feel it appropriate to give back to the community. The entire staff is behind this and it motivates them. I believe that this is because everyone wants to be part of something larger than they are.

I also tithe from my personal income to different groups/people outside of my company. It helps to create a larger positive effect and I believe it is part of my personal mission; "To contribute to the well-being and the collective knowledge of humankind." It allows me to also feel that I am contributing to something larger than I am.

- Dr. Barton Goldsmith

If you own a business, you pay yourself a salary, right? Because you are the owner, that doesn't mean things are any different than if it was a conglomerate – you tithe your salary – your personal income."

- Daphne Hill

n paying our 10% tithe, we are acknowledging that we have God as our business partner. You can't have a better partner than Him. At every turn, He has been there and we are so thankful for the opportunities we have had to see His hand in our business.

- Julie Larson

I believe a business should act ethically, be socially responsible, and make decisions and, occasionally, donate to the community which nourishes it. But I don't think it becomes a tithing issue until it becomes the private property of an individual. You becomes the private property of an individual. You owe God your best effort in your work, but if you tithe from business profits you take income and benefits away from your employees that may be crucial to their well-being.

- Karen J. Murphy-Linden

Should I tithe in secret or in the open?

👆 Tithing is a private affair. Let your conscience be your guide as to whether you want to witness to others about tithing. If it makes you feel good to share your tithing experiences with spiritually awakened others, do it. If you talk about tithing before the spiritually unenlightened, they may ridicule you, laugh or belittle you, which could ultimately steal away the joy and magnificence you feel in your tithing benefits.

One of the richest men on earth (who lived to be 100), W. Clement Stone, had a magnificent obsession to be America's greatest philanthropist and tither. He did a tremendous amount of good and constantly encouraged others to do likewise. When Dr. Robert Schuller interviewed W. Clement Stone about how it feels to be really rich, Stone answered, "It gives me the power to do even greater good in many different places at the same time. Every person has the ability to create good. I am cheering you on and challenging you to do it. I dare you to give!"

How do I encourage my kids to tithe?

👆 It's important that you start teaching your kids about the wonders of tithing as soon as possible. In my household, my girls grew up with tithing and

To explain the tithing concept to our young children, we told them about angels who live on earth and help others. We let them know that anyone can be an angel. At Christmas, we told them that with all of the gifts under the tree, perhaps we needed to be angels too. They each took five gifts from under the tree and we all delivered them together to children less fortunate. It's an experience that has stayed with them and a tradition we continue.

- Sheryl Herrera

"gratitude giving" stories in their heads. As they began to do their chores for allowance, they were told to give ten cents to God and ten cents to savings before they spent anything else. Obviously as young adults, they got to add taxes to that total picture! (Even Jesus said, *"Pay unto Caesar that which is Caesar's."*) My girls have consistently and religiously maintained this practice ever since. The sooner you begin, the more automatic it becomes.

At all holidays, inspire your children to have generous hearts. At Christmas, have them make one gift for some less privileged person. At

Valentine's Day, deliver heart cookies to a shut-in. At Thanksgiving Day, be sure to invite someone to dinner who has no where to go.

What is the best tithing demonstration you've ever heard?

෪ Three come to mind immediately:

1. John Crean, founder and CEO of Fleetwood International, publicly gave (tithed) $12 million dollars worth of Rancho Capistrano, California stock to Dr. Robert Schuller's ministry. Fleetwood stock jumped three times the same day because the U.S. Government simultaneously announced that they were putting a lot of money into modular housing, which is Fleetwood's specialty. You may call this a coincidence. I don't think so.

I heard Mr. Crean interviewed by Dr. Schuller and he stated that when he was young, a friend told him that in life, "There are winners and losers. Winners are givers, and losers are takers." He chose to be a winner and he now tithes 50% of his gross income.

2. I've already mentioned Dave Anderson, who co-founded the Rain Forest Café and Famous Dave's BBQ Rib companies. He does Reverse Tithing – where he keeps 10% and gives 90% away.

3. The Bill and Linda Gates Foundation was created in January of 2000 through the merger of the Gates Learning Foundation, which focused on expanding access to technology through public libraries, and the William H. Gates Foundation, which focused on improving global health. With Bill Gates personally leading its funding, the foundation now has an endowment of approximately $24 billion. In its first full year of activity (2001) it gave more than $1 billion in grants to more than 2,050 grantees all over the world through its Global Health,Education, Library and Pacific Northwest divisions.

This is a stellar example of a very gifted individual who utilized his talents to change and challenge the world for the better…then took earnings from that gift to philanthropically begin changing the world, too. Can you imagine how much $1 billion in "seed money" per year can do for this world?

I challenge you to become a billionaire and give most of it away! In the book, *The One Minute Millionaire*, we teach that if you save one dollar for 66 years at no interest, you've got $25,000 to your name. But if you save that same amount at 10% interest, you grow $2.75 million instead. "Compounding," Einstein said, "Is the eighth wonder of the world." Indeed! Think of the tithing you can do because of compounded interest!

Chapter Four

To Whom Do I Tithe?

I just heard about tithing.
To whom should I give?

❧ When I wrote my first version of *The Miracle of Tithing*, I instructed my readers to give solely to a "spiritual group that resonates positively and constructively with what your beliefs are." (Meaning churches, synagogues, temples, ashrams, mosques, etc.) I want this tithing concept to have the broadest appeal and most comprehensive reach ever. Giving is giving, whether it's done via Christianity, Judaism, Islam, Buddhism, Hinduism…whatever.

I still firmly believe that your spiritual organization of choice is a perfect selection for your tithing purpose as it serves you and greatly serves others.

First, if you're not an active, participating church attendee, visit a variety of churches and choose the minister, not the church building, not the denomination, not necessarily what your parents did, or what someone else said. Be still and listen to your inner-knower. Your inner knower will tell you what is right for you, in the quiet stillness of your prayer, meditation and spiritual retreats.

Choose the minister, priest or Rabbi who leads you to ever greater and deeper spiritual truth, wisdom and understanding.

A great and inspiring teacher or preacher can lead your personal growth, development and fulfillment to new heights. Once you've located your spiritual mentor, support him or her financially, mentally, spiritually, emotionally and even physically. Befriend your spiritual spigot of enlightenment, enlivenment, and enrichment. Attend church and its many activities, volunteer your assistance, take classes, and go to spiritual retreats, conventions and growth meetings. Your life will blossom and bloom in magnificent new ways.

One final suggestion: Make sure your choice of ministers or spiritual teachers has great plans to do phenomenal amounts of good to the benefit of all humanity. If they are on the grow, you will be also.

I believe the entire universe is God's "church." Can I tithe to a non-profit organization or foundation?

∽ Insofar as God is omni-present throughout the universe, and insofar that he commanded us to be stewards of the creation He's provided us, it's better to give to non-profit organizations and foundations than to not give at all. Giving is giving. Jesus said, *"Give and it will be given unto you."* Jesus did not say where to give, but that giving of itself is the gift.

Where is your passion? What do you love

more than anything on this created planet?

One of the writers who works with me was raised in church all her life. She has great respect and love for the foundation it has created in her life and enjoys her growing, personal relationship with God. At the same time, she sees God's hand in the abundance we have in nature and, when she talks about tigers, her eyes well with tears. Working to keep this magnificent beast from extinction is her tithing passion, and she tithes most of her business and personal funds to www.tigeraid.org. Each time income arrives, she writes another check. She told me recently that they called her from their headquarters, exclaiming over the sheer number of checks they were receiving. The checks aren't hefty, by any means, but they're consistently delivered and – my guess is – showing up more often as her business grows in abundance.

My dear friend Wyland (www.wyland.com), the world's leading marine artist, is wildly passionate about the creatures in the sea. Not only does his foundation provide education and conservation resources to save our phenomenal creatures of the sea, but he personally tithes a great deal of his personal income (including that from the incredible "Whaling Walls" he paints around the world) to the saving, cleaning and salvaging of our oceans. He tells me, "If people see the beauty in nature, they will work to preserve it." Wyland

plans to paint a 10-mile length of The Great
Wall of China just before the 2008 Olympics to
further awaken the world's people to the needs of
our oceans.

What do you see? What do you want to save?
Get excited, get behind it, and start providing that
tithing "seed" that begins an endless flow. If you
don't stand for something, you'll fall for anything.

Can I give to the hungry and the poor as a tithe? If I give to relatives in need, is that a tithe?

✍ Jesus said, "That which you have done to the
least of my children, you have done unto me."
Therefore, it is good to aid and assist the hungry
and the poor in need.

I just ask you to use one measuring stick
against this: Are you giving them a handout or a
hand up? If you're giving them a handout, I don't
believe this is a tithe. While it helps them in the
short term, in many cases, it's not being acted upon
as a "seed" that primes the flow of abundance in
their lives. It is, instead, allowing them to stay at
the same level of co-dependence for a longer period
of time.

A hand-up is a different matter. Earlier in the
book, one of our readers wrote about giving $2,500

to a woman who'd been stolen from and needed the money to pay employees for work they'd already done. In my eyes, this is almost a "pay it forward" mentality that has people helping other people out of crisis. But, just like in the movie, **Pay it Forward**, ask whomever you give to that they, in turn, pay it forward when they can afford to do so.

My friend, Nido Queben, came to America from Lebanon with five dollars in his pocket and no English skills. Because of assistance and a scholarship, he has become phenomenally successful as a speaker and businessman. He has promised to pay forward the scholarship that he received, and asks others to help him help thousands of students who possess similar dreams of new life and success.

1. If possible, help them learn the principles so they can then help themselves. Remember the oft-quoted phrase, "If you feed a person a fish you feed him/her for a day. If you teach a person to fish, you feed him/her for a lifetime."

I have known several individuals who have been so inspired and helped by the ideas in Napoleon Hill's book, **Think and Grow Rich**, that they individually have given thousands of copies to others in hopes that they will learn these principles in a useable way. Likewise, many have read this, bought copies and given them to their church libraries. One visionary leader bought 5,000 copies and gave them to each member of his church. Later, he reported that the tithes had more than doubled.

In a magazine interview in *Personal Selling Power* (March 1983) my friend Dr. Wayne Dyer said, "There are a lot of things I do because I feel they are helpful to other people. I see myself as a giver. I give a lot of money to charity. I spend a lot of my time helping unfortunate people learn the tithing principles and showing them empirically, through recognition of their own demonstration, that it works."

Meanwhile, Wayne continues to experience great publishing success with more than 70 million books sold. Amazingly, he reports that they virtually "write themselves in days." I believe that tithers move to a new level of consciousness, awareness and growth.

Reaching others by teaching others will enrich you and the world. If everyone learned and practiced tithing, there would be no more lack of any kind.

2. While your finances will always help the poor and needy, remember that you can also tithe your time and service to helping them get back on track. Axiomatically, there is an old cliché that says, "If you need something, give some of it away." So, if you need money, give money tithes. If you need time, give some of your time to a church, mission, or hospital. Read to the blind, join Meals on Wheels or Big Brothers or Sisters and offer your time, talents and service.

Does putting away money for your child's future college education count?

❧ No. This is a great demonstration of your financial responsibility and hope/expectation for your child's future, but I do not believe this is a tithe.

I have very little income to tithe. Can I tithe service instead?

❧ Absolutely. In fact, many ministers and non-profit organizations have told me that they desperately need people to give of their talents, service and time. One of our books, *Chicken Soup for the Volunteer's Soul*, is dedicated to America's 200 million selfless volunteers. The stories will touch your heart and soul and allow you to feel the true nobility of your own service.

Remember, the key to all tithing is the fact that you're recognizing your one source of supply … you're grateful for the abundance you have in your life…and you're giving back joyfully with a loving, appreciative heart. Anything you can do to serve others is a boost to the way this universe works and, ultimately, provides an energetic, enlivening boost to *you*.

Two words of caution when you commit to tithing your service.

1. Make it a solid commitment. Decide exactly what you will do, write it down and stick to it. Don't use "service" as an excuse to not tithe income.

2. Every year, increase the amount of service, just as you would a money tithe from increased income. Bob Hope invested his comedic and organizational genius in creating the WSO. Each year, he pointedly increased his service in this regard until he'd raised more than $1 billion for charities around the world.

Likewise, Jerry Lewis' telethons raised the bar again by raising more than $4 billion dollars. Thomas Edison once said, "If you do all you can do, you will literally astonish yourself." More needs to be done. Only you can roll up your sleeves and do what you can do.

After my wife died, my life stopped. I didn't work for a year and couldn't really function. I took a workshop (and later worked) with Elizabeth Kubler-Ross MD and author of On Death and Dying. *She introduced me to "hospice" and I found it to be the hardest and yet most rewarding work of my life. Though I was paid very little for doing grief counseling with hospice families, I donated all the money back. Not long after I returned to regular counseling, other doors opened and I became one of those 'self-made millionaires' you write about. I know it is a direct result of the work I did, giving both my time and money to those who needed it more than I.*

- Dr. Barton Goldsmith

Just two comments about this beautiful story. First, Mr. Goldsmith was hit with grief and, in most cases, when you're grieving; you're immobilized with fear. I told you earlier in this book that I think God gives us fear so that we'll push through it. In this case, Mr. Goldsmith DID push through and, even better, may not have even recognized that he helped many families apply the same skill as he learned and worked as a grief counselor with them.

Secondly, once he began serving (without pay, too), he started to open up again. While he may have healed in the interim between loss and taking on the counseling, it's my bet that his healing occurred in the time he provided the counseling service to those in similar situations. He opened his heart, was filled with passion for his work and, as a result, was eventually rewarded.

From My Readers

Tithing goes beyond giving money. You can tithe your ideas, talents, love, time...the options are endless but equally beneficial. First you have to plant the seeds, and then you will reap the fruits. There is always a "first," which constitutes an action, and there is always a "result." But first, you must take action, no matter how small, take action.

- Lisa Vaden

I also tithe my time and talents, meaning that I consistently give of my time and donate whatever talent I can to help. I volunteer within the community for several organizations.

I don't actually track my time – that is not the

spirit of tithing. I just live with the idea that I need to give every day in some way. I have been blessed to serve people in all walks of life. If someone needs a favor, I can be counted upon to help.

I have found that the more I share my talents freely, the more I have. It is amazing to me. People ask how I do so much and I answer that it is because I have a testimony of giving.

- Debbi Stumpf

Before my wife, Darlene, and I got married we agreed that we would have eight children. After our sixth was born we couldn't have any more biological children so we thought we would adopt the last two. There were so many "unadoptable children" needing homes that we opened our home to some of them.

To make a long story short, we ended up with fourteen beautiful, handicapped, adopted kids. (For a total of 20!) I had just started a new business and we were blessed with great success. We always had more than enough to go around. In retrospect, I guess we were tithing by taking in kids from third world countries and California and caring for them. But we never looked at it that way.

- Al Hartman

Fifteen years ago I hit rock bottom. I became involved with a twelve-step fellowship, which focuses on recovery from addiction to drugs. In that program, I was told that I couldn't keep it unless I gave it away. I tithe each time the basket goes around, but the main focus of my giving is in performing a service to my community.

I volunteer my time at Juvenile Hall because God says that's where I need to be. I can be found on most Saturday nights at the hall with my kids. Some of them are as young as ten years old, and sometimes it makes me very sad. I share my experience with them and sometimes I read them a Chicken Soup for the Soul story and we laugh . Sometimes, they even hear the message, "You don't ever have to come back here."

Years ago, I sat in a meeting and heard a friend share "When I am being of service, everything in my life is taken care of." In my experience I have not had to do without anything I've needed for the last fifteen years. Today I know that "My job is to go about my Father's business and His job is to take care of me.

- Jeff Hernandez

Chapter Five

Problems and Issues with Tithing

Many of my readers have written to me with questions about their specific tithing challenges. Some of their questions are here, along with my answers – which are strictly opinions, gleaned from my experience and understanding of tithing.

What if I'm living on savings without income? Should I tithe?

ꙮ All I can tell you is what I've done from personal experience. When Patty and I had to get a loan to live on, we tithed 10% immediately.

Earlier in this book, one of the readers stated that she tithes on all the money she draws from her business income. Given these two examples, I'd suggest tithing only on what you draw from savings to live on. If you're uncomfortable tithing a full 10%, then tithe what you can, even if it's 1%. Again, I don't know if your savings is at $42.09 or if it's in a six-figure range…so, this is a decision you need to make by relying on your "inner knower."

My husband was laid off and we barely have enough to live on, much less to pay the bills. Should we tithe?

ꙮ Of course! To overcome lack and poverty consciousness and enter into prosperity you absolutely NEED to tithe. Tithing will expand your awareness and keep the disease of poverty at bay. Speak your word to your bills; speak your word to get perfect employment and total enjoyment from life.

If you really have a lot of fear about starting, do as my minister and her husband did when they began tithing: They started tithing a percentage, just a little extra outside their "comfort level." In this case, it was 3% of their gross income. As the channels of abundance opened up, they increased the percentage of tithing. Each time they would feel comfortable, they would increase their tithing another percentage point until they reached the desired 10%.

After five years, they increased their tithe to more than 10%. You can do the same or more!

If my cash flow is really tight, is it a "violation" to skip a week of tithing if it means bills will go unpaid?

  There are several possible answers. Read the following with feeling and you will hear what you need to hear now:

The Bible clearly states that you should tithe "first fruits" then pay your bills. By tithing first, your tight cash flow will become loose in unexpected ways. I believe this is because you're walking through fear with faith and you will be duly rewarded for that faith. *The Prayer of Jabez* by Dr. Bruce Wilkinson says, "Daily, you should ask for, expect, get and be bountifully thankful for your blessings." His anecdote on asking for blessings will guarantee change in your behavior as you, in turn, begin to recognize and show gratitude for your blessings.

Whether you tithe or you don't tithe, you still have to pay your bills. Bills are, for the most part, a constant in our lives. Tithing or not tithing, however, can actually work in conjunction with – or completely against – that constant. By tithing as prescribed repeatedly in the Bible, you literally **open the floodgates of heaven** to attend to your needs. If you don't tithe, you shut off this invisible system and miss out on your deserved blessings.

Should I wait until the recession is over to start tithing?

No, it is more vital that you begin tithing now more than ever. To end your personal recession, you've been encouraged to start tithing at once, using whatever resources you have right here and right now. Tithing will facilitate the automatic improvement of your situation and circumstances. Note that the greater your need, the more important it is to start tithing immediately. One's problems all emanate from one's mental attitude,

During these hard times, we have increased our level of giving. Why? Because others have decreased theirs. The non-profits about which we care need people to make up for those who decrease their giving. We learned this in a lesson before we got married. A man spoke with us about how he and his wife increased their level of giving during the Great Depression. The IRS sent a man out to investigate, for surely anyone who increased their giving at THAT time was doing something illegal.

After two weeks of investigation, they left empty-handed and never bothered him again. I figure if he and his wife could increase their giving during the Depression, we can do the same in these days. Will we get anything back for doing this? Perhaps, but we don't care. That's not why we do it.

- Don Shelton

disposition, mood and beliefs. The richest man in Hawaii once told me, "Your attitude determines your budget."

The very same principle applies to the

recession "out there." To end recession around the world, we should all be tithing with whatever resources we have right here and right now. Spiritually done, tithing (done with your soul, heart and head) always gets the desired result.

Earlier in this book, I wrote about a frozen pond of water wherein there is no movement of that water. As soon as the tiniest thaw begins on the edges, though, water begins to move into motion and its energetic state begins to speed up the thawing process. When we tithe, we're thawing the edges of a frozen, recessionary state. Once that thaw begins, energy moves into motion and we move at an accelerated state out of recessionary mode.

Should I feel guilty about not tithing to this point?

∽ "Guilt" – Random House Dictionary defines as "a feeling of remorse or responsibility for some offense, crime or wrong, whether real or imagined."

Why would you want to be stuck there? Feelings of guilt are counter-productive to your own greater good. Guilt is a form of self-persecution and has no positive pay-off. If you have not tithed, don't feel guilty about it. What's done is done.

However, the day is still young! I want you to

try it – for six months as a trial only. Do it consistently, don't let up and stick to it. You'll be amazed at the emotions that come to take the place of any guilt or remorse you've felt from the past.

What if you tithe and your spouse doesn't?

❦ This was one of the top three questions my readers asked of me! I suggest you tithe from your own personal income, leading by example. Don't harp on it; don't force them into doing something they don't want to do. As we've mentioned earlier in the book, if you give grudgingly, you're better off not giving at all. So, do your part, send it away joyfully, and let your story show your partner the truth in its own time and in its own way.

From My Readers

Give what you can and pray for the other to come to their senses!

- Bob & Debbie Demaria

I would not expect him to live by my principles until he accepts them as the truth.

- Donna Gulley

After I read your e-book The Miracle of Tithing (first edition) I knew it was time to tithe. My husband was not particularly enthralled with the idea, yet he didn't come right out and say, "No." After discussing the pros and cons, I offered your book to him as an option to read. From that point, he was ready to begin tithing. He's always been a really giving guy with his time while being much more conservative of his hard-earned dollars. With tithing, I can see that he now really enjoys sharing his money too. I feel tithing has brought us closer together in that we actually discuss consciously who we want to help financially each month.

- Dru Bloomfield

Tithe only from your salary, the money that you have earned. Let him/her know that you will be tithing from the money you've earned. Love your husband/wife and never bring the subject of tithing up again. Your generous way of being and results that show up in your life will do all of your speaking.

- Michel-Joy DelRe

Perhaps a challenge or test could be proposed: Let's tithe for a period of time, and see what happens." I'm sure that it will be found that there will be enough money to go around, either through less expenses, or more income.

- Eric Ackley

Through Harv Ecker's class, we learned to break out money for each partner before the money is allocated to the family financial structure. If one partner wants to donate, then they will have their own personal funds to do so plus, they do not have to be accountable to their partner for it. It has worked so well for us. We have been able to carry that into other financial responsibilities as well.

- Jeanie Abeel

Been there, done that. She now tithes IDEAS, something we picked up from you. She gives time to solve problems for small agencies, not realizing she is tithing, and truth be told, her time is worth more than her money would be to these people. If a spouse doesn't want to tithe "family income" then compromise and give 5% money and 5% time to one of HER worthy causes.

- Gordon Alexander

One can/should make a decision over what one DIRECTLY earns and controls, not what another DIRECTLY earns or controls. So the question becomes, for example, what about the wife who is a believer when (a) the husband is not a believer, (b) the husband is the sole "bread winner," and (c) the husband does not believe in tithing or supporting the concept of tithing? In this case, the wife should be allowed to tithe after the merging of family funds. After the merging, the wife has influence or control over household funds. Whatever amount of funds the wife has control over can be used as a foundation for tithing. Additionally – tithing should never be an issue for division. If tithing becomes a division, then it is not of God, for God is not divisive.

- Melwyn Hallam

You tithe what God gives YOU. Your spouse is growing just as you are. Your rates of growth are simply different. Even if your spouse has not grown to the point of tithing, the compromise should be that you tithe YOUR income. God put the two of you together. Help your mate by letting him/her grow at his/her own pace. Understand the concept of the growth process and talk it out with God and then your mate.

- Daphne Hill

Thank goodness I don't have this problem.
If I did, I think I'd "pony up" my partner's share anyway.

- Charlie Roth

There is an old saying, "There's more than one way to skin a cat." So be creative, give through creativity. Why do you think we're such intelligent creatures...to just follow directions? We have free choice, creative minds, and generous spirits. Just put those three things together and start giving. You'll be led to the when, where and how of it.

- Donna J. Long

Conclusion

❧ Thank you for expressing the interest, curiosity, and faith to pick up this book and read it for yourself. In just the re-creation and updating of the book alone, I've been humbled and honored with the stories I've read, the open hearts I've witnessed, and the sheer generosity of spirit that drives thousands upon thousands of consistent tithers in this world of ours. We are shifting the world for the better. It's my fervent hope that you'll be joining us.

In my introduction, I promised you "bookend" stories that came from readers who tell the true tale of miraculous tithing.

Here's the final story:

From My Readers

Giving Back to God

A couple of years ago I was having a hard time financially. It had been a slow year for business; I'd had some big medical bills; and I had not been as careful with my money as I should have been. It was November, and I didn't know how I was going to make it through the end of the year.

I called my friend Anna to ask her advice.

She had a good head for money. I tearfully explained my predicament. She listened quietly, was kind and sympathetic, completely understanding. She did not judge or scold.

"You want my advice?" she asked, when I had finished telling her my sad story. "Well, sure," I replied, "that's why I called you."

Tithe," she said simply.

I couldn't believe my ears. "You don't understand," I objected. "I just told you I don't have any money coming in, I've got all these bills piled up, and I don't know how I'm going to meet the mortgage next month. I can't tithe – I have nothing to tithe with!"

"Well, you asked my advice, and I'm giving it to you," she said matter-of-factly. "All I have to share with you is my own experience. If you start to tithe, you shift your relationship with God. It is an act of faith in which you essentially say, 'I know I will be taken care of, so I can give this money back to God.' It works for me and it works for lots of other people I know, too."

I knew in my heart Anna was right. Tithing was something I had wanted to do for a long time, but I was afraid – afraid I would not have enough money to meet my needs, afraid to give away 10% of my income, afraid of financial insecurity. I had heard other people talk about tithing in the past, and being a spiritual person, I liked the idea - but my fear always got the better of me.

"Here's what I'd suggest," Anna continued, "Why don't you call Naomi and ask her what her experience has been with tithing. Then decide if it's right for you."

I thanked Anna for her advice, and immediately dialed Naomi's number. She was more than happy to tell me about her experience with tithing. She had been in similar financial straits a few years earlier, and Anna had given her the same advice she'd given me. Reluctantly, Naomi agreed to do it.

She started by tithing to a twelve-step community of which she was a member, because Anna had instructed her to "give to the spiritual community that nurtures you." Naomi took a check to the office of this twelve-step program every time she got paid (she was self-employed in the real estate business). "The first time I tithed," Naomi told me, "I sold a $400,000 house the very next week! I'm sure it was a direct result of my tithing."

After a while, Anna suggested that Naomi start tithing to her local synagogue, since she had been born and raised Jewish. "I'm not going to do that," Naomi protested. "I lost my faith years ago, and I'm not going to give them any money."

Anna nudged Naomi, "Just try it. Do it a few times. See what happens."

So the next time Naomi received a paycheck, she drove to the synagogue and gave them a check. Before long, the rabbi invited her to come to a special event at the synagogue. She went. She met a few people she liked, and she started going to more events. Her heart began softening toward the Jewish faith, and over time she gradually felt a part of this community.

About this time, her young nephew turned thirteen and it was time for his Bar Mitzvah. She knew that her sister didn't have much money, so Naomi offered to pay for the event. Naomi had been estranged from her sister, but she loved her nephew very much, and she wanted to do this for him. Over the months of planning the ceremony and the party, Naomi and her sister gradually worked through their differences and were reconciled. The Bar Mitzvah was a wonderful day for the whole family.

In short, Naomi's commitment to tithe 10% of whatever she earned transformed her life. Tithing did more than put her on sound financial ground. It brought her back to her Jewish faith, it strengthened the bond between her and her nephew, and it reunited her with her sister. She was living a life of miracles. If I had any doubt about the efficacy of tithing, it disappeared in listening to Naomi's story.

Tithing means acknowledging that no matter how little one has, there are always other people who are worse off. Tithing means saying to God, "I trust that you will provide for me, and Iam willing to give back 10% to do your work in the world."

Tithing lifts the burden of fear from my heart, and replaces it with trust. Tithing to a spiritual organization that gives me spiritual sustenance is the best way of saying "thanks" for all that I have received.
once heard Jack Canfield (co-author of Chicken Soup for the Soul) talk about tithing and its role in his life. He said, "Both my co-author (Mark Victor Hansen) and I have been tithing for many years and we think it's an important part of our business success. (Their Chicken Soup for the Soul books have sold over 80 millions copies!)

I've been tithing for two years now, ever since the phone conversations I had with Anna and Naomi. I don't sell real estate, and I haven't had the success of Chicken Soup for the Soul, but my finances have stabilized and the peace of mind I feel is wonderful. Tithing shifted my relationship to God from one of "fearful child asking God's protection" to "adult partner with God" in doing good in the world. It feels wonderful.

BJ Gallagher Hateley
from **Everything I Need to Know
I Learned from Other Women.**

About the Author

Mark Victor Hansen

❧ In the area of human potential, no one is better known and more respected than Mark Victor Hansen. For more than 28 years he has influenced society's top leaders and the general public on a global scale, helping people and organizations, from all walks of life, reshape their personal vision of what's possible.

His credentials include a lifetime of entrepreneurial successes, in addition to an extensive academic background.

Mark is the co-author of the wildly successful *Chicken Soup for the Soul*® series. His newest book, *The One Minute Millionaire: The Enlightened Way to Wealth,* is destined to inspire the creation of one million new millionaires this decade who will contribute one million dollars to the charity or church of their choice.

Mark is the recipient of the prestigious Horatio Alger Award for his extraordinary life achievements and giving heart. He is also known as a passionate philanthropist and humanitarian, working for organizations such as Habitat for Humanity, The American Red Cross, The March of Dimes, Childhelp USA and many others.

Mark is an enthusiastic crusader of what's possible, driven to make the world a better place.

Services Offered

~ Mark's powerful messages of possibility, opportunity and action have helped create startling change in thousands of organizations worldwide.

Speaking to conventions and organizations all over the world, Mark offers keynote presentations and seminars that build on the principles of his bestselling books and audio programs.

For further information about Mark Victor Hansen's programs, please contact:

Mark Victor Hansen & Associates
P.O. Box 7665
Newport Beach, CA 92658-7665
(800) 433-2314
(949) 764-2640
(949) 722-6912 fax

Share The Miracle of Tithing with Others

Give the gift of giving!

✍ Additional copies of *The Miracle of Tithing* are available for $9.95.

Order today by calling (800) 433-2314 or visit www.markvictorhansen.com

Quantity discounts available!

If you are interested in ordering multiple copies for your stewardship, pledge and/or commitment programs for your congregation, please contact:

Mark Victor Hansen & Associates, Inc.
(800) 433-2314
(949) 764-2640
(949) 722-6912 fax
service@markvictorhansen.com

Other Works by Mark Victor Hansen

Books

The One Minute Millionaire:
The Enlightened Way to Wealth

The ever-expanding *Chicken Soup for the Soul* series

The Power of Focus

Future Diary

The Aladdin Factor: How to Ask for
and Get Everything You Want

Dare to Win

Treasury of Quotes

Out of the Blue, Delight Comes into Our Lives

Audio Programs

Dreams Don't Have Deadlines

How to Think Bigger Than
You Ever Thought You Could Think

The Aladdin Factor

Mastermind Your Way to Millions

Sell Yourself Rich

MEGA Book Marketing University

Special Reports & E-Booklets

Creating the Dream Team Advantage

Story-Board Your Future

There's No Such Thing as Failure

How to Veer from the Beaten Path

Focus on Your Primary Aim

Rejecting Rejection

Available for purchase at
www.markvictorhansen.com
Or by calling (800) 433-2314

Make the Rest of Your Life
the BEST of Your Life!

Dreams Don't Have Deadlines
Living Your Dreams
No Matter What Your Age!

❧ It's time to refresh, revitalize, and rethink the concept of age and success. It's time to see your age in a new light – and realize it can be a stepping stone to achieving "fulfilling" success. With *Dreams Don't Have Deadlines*, you'll find an abundance of practical tips to get you started, worksheets to help you identify your goals, meditations and exercises to keep you on track, and heart-warming stories to inspire you.

No one knows more about making dreams come true than MARK VICTOR HANSEN. Yet Mark did not achieve anything close to this level of success until he was well into his 40s. How did he finally do it? He knew that dreams don't have a deadline - and once you've heard this exciting and inspiring program, you'll know it too!

Order today: www.markvictorhansen.com
or by calling: (800) 433-2314

6 Audiocassettes/Workbook $~~$60~~ $65
6 Compact Discs/Workbook $~~$79~~ $75

Anything is Possible
IF You Dare to Ask

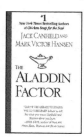

The Aladdin Factor
How to Ask for, and Get, Everything You Want

❦ It's an important process business and industry leaders have already learned and want to impart to you. And, it's a concept you'll use everyday to move outside your comfort zone and seize the prosperity, fulfillment and happiness you deserve. The Aladdin Factor is a practical guide for taking control of your life, realizing better business and personal relationships, having and giving more love, maximizing your talents and skills and enriching your lifestyle like never before.

You'll learn not only how to ask for what you want, but how to ask and what to ask for. You'll discover the five barriers we all face in asking for what we want and how to overcome them?and you'll read about the seven characteristics of those who ask successfully.

Available at bookstores everywhere!
ISBN 0-425-15075-5 $13.00
Order today: www.markvictorhansen.com
or by calling: (800) 433-2314

More from the
Chicken Soup for the Soul ® series!

Each one of these NEW heartwarming titles
will bring inspiration both to you
and the loved ones in your life...

*Chicken Soup for
the Romantic Soul*
$12.95

*Chicken Soup for
the the Grieving Soul*
$12.95

*Chicken Soup Cartoons
for Moms*
$12.95

*Chicken Soup for
the Mother and Daughter Soul*
$12.95

A Over 55 titles to choose from...
Order today: www.markvictorhansen.com
or by calling: (800) 433-2314
Also available at bookstores everywhere!